INTERFACE

THE BOOK AND DISK THAT WORK TOGETHER

ROMANS

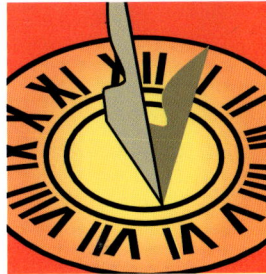

World Book

in association with

TWOCAN

Published in the United States and Canada by
World Book, Inc.
525 W. Monroe Street, Chicago, IL 60661, USA

ISBN: 0-7166-7217-0 (Mac)
ISBN: 0-7166-7216-2 (PC)
ISBN: 0-7166-7215-4 (CD)

For information on other World Book products, call 1-800-255-1750, x 2238,
or visit us at our Web site at http://www.worldbook.com.

Created by
Two-Can Publishing Ltd,
346 Old Street, London, EC1V 9NQ

Disk
Creative Director: Jason Page
Programming Director: Paul Steven
Art Director: Sarah Evans
Designer: James Evans
Assistant Editor: Lyndall Thomas
Programmer: Colette McFadden
Consultant: Emma Dench
Illustrators: Jeffrey Lewis, Carlo Tartalia,
Jon Stuart, Alan Rowe
Project Manager: Joya Bart-Plange
U.S. Editor: Karen Ingebretsen, World Book Publishing

Book
Creative Director: Jason Page
Assistant Editor: Lyndall Thomas
Author: Peter Crisp
Designer: Michele Egar
Consultant: Emma Dench
Project Manager: Joya Bart-Plange
U.S. Editor: Karen Ingebretsen, World Book Publishing

Photograph Credits: front cover Ancient Art and Architecture Collection,
p. 11 Zefa, p. 13 E.T. Archive, p. 13 (top right) Ancient Art and Architecture Collection,
p. 14 Ancient Art and Architecture Collection, p. 16 Michael Holford, p. 17 C.M. Dixon,
p. 18 (top right) C.M. Dixon, p. 18 (bottom right) Bridgeman Art Library, p. 20 Michael Holford,
p. 21 Bruce Coleman, p. 23 (top left) Ancient Art and Architecture Collection,
p. 23 (bottom) Michael Holford, p. 24 Ancient Art and Architecture Collection,
p. 25 (top left) C.M. Dixon, p. 25 (bottom right) Bridgeman Art Library,
p. 27 Bridgeman Art Library, p. 28 Michael Holford, p. 34 (left) Michael Holford,
p. 34 (top right) Michael Holford, p. 34 (bottom right) Bruce Coleman, p. 35 Bruce Coleman
Illustration Credits: pp. 8-28 Gillian Hunt, pp. 29-33 Maxine Hamil

1 2 3 4 5 6 7 8 9 10 01 00 99 98

INTERFACT

INTERFACT will have you hooked in minutes – and that's a fact!

● **The disk is filled with interactive activities, puzzles, quizzes, and games that are fun to do and packed with interesting facts.**

See if you would make a good Roman citizen in an interactive adventure story.

You decide to go witness the excitement of a gladiator contest!

But where will you find the gladiator games?

● At the Colosseum
● At the Circus Maximus

Click on the answer

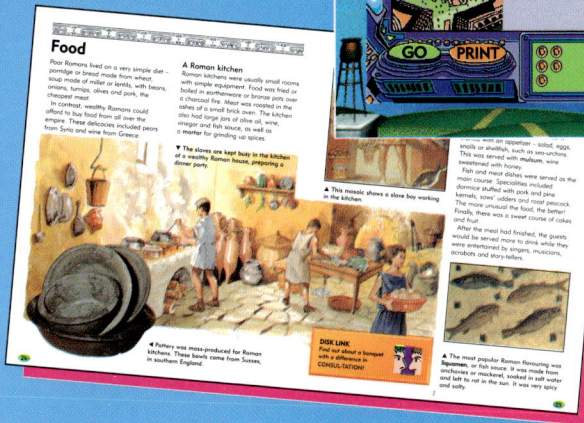

GO   PRINT

Food

Poor Romans lived on a very simple diet – porridge or bread made from wheat, soup made of millet or lentils, with beans, onions, turnips, olives and pork, the cheapest meat.

In contrast, wealthy Romans could afford to buy food from all over the empire. These delicacies included pears from Syria and wine from Greece.

A Roman kitchen
Roman kitchens were usually small rooms with simple equipment. Food was fried or boiled in earthenware or bronze pots over a charcoal fire. Meat was roasted in the ashes of a small brick oven. The kitchen also had large jars of olive oil, wine, vinegar and fish sauce, as well as a mortar for grinding up spices.

▼ The slaves are kept busy in the kitchen of a wealthy Roman house, preparing a dinner party.

▲ This mosaic shows a slave boy working in the kitchen.

...with an appetizer – salad, eggs, snails or shellfish, such as sea-urchins. This was served with mulsum, wine sweetened with honey.

Fish and meat dishes were served as the main course. Specialities included dormice stuffed with pork and pine kernels, sows' udders and roast peacock. The more unusual the food, the better! Finally, there was a sweet course of cakes and fruit.

After the meal had finished, the guests would be served more to drink while they were entertained by singers, musicians, acrobats and story-tellers.

DISK LINK
Find out about a banquet with a difference in CONSUL-TATION!

▲ *Pottery was mass-produced for Roman kitchens. These bowls came from Sussex, in southern England.*

▲ The most popular Roman flavouring was liquamen, or fish sauce. It was made from anchovies or mackerel, soaked in salt water and left to rot in the sun. It was very spicy and salty.

Discover what the Romans ate and how they cooked their food.

● **Open the book and discover more fascinating information highlighted with lots of full-color illustrations and photographs.**

● To get the most out of **INTERFACT,** use the book and disk together. Look for the special signs called Disk Links and Bookmarks. To find out more, turn to page 43.

23

BOOKMARK

DISK LINK VIII
Why not spend some time at the baths? You can when you HIT THE TOWN!

Once you've launched **INTERFACT,** you'll never look back.

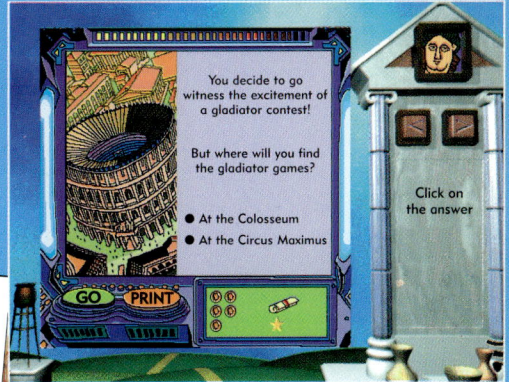

LOAD UP!
Go to **page 40** to find out how to load your disk and click into action.

What's on the disk

HELP SCREEN

Learn how to use the disk in no time at all.

Welcome to the
INTERFACT
disk on Romans

To look at all the different things on the disk, simply click the arrow keys with your mouse.

As you do this, you'll see a description of each activity in the text box.

Click on the picture at the top of the screen to select the activity you want to investigate.

These are the controls that the Help Screen will tell you how to use:
- arrow keys
- text boxes
- "hot" words

MIX AND MATCH

Learn about emperors, slaves, soldiers, gladiators, and more!

What a mix-up! The heads, bodies, and legs of all sorts of people from ancient Rome have been jumbled up. Sort them out, then find out more about each person.

TIME TREK

Set off on a journey of discovery through the history of ancient Rome.

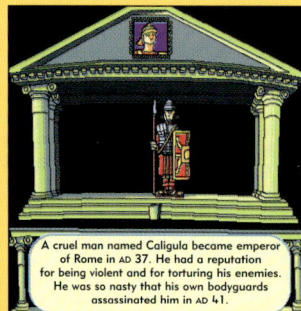

A cruel man named Caligula became emperor of Rome in AD 37. He had a reputation for being violent and for torturing his enemies. He was so nasty that his own bodyguards assassinated him in AD 41.

Take a trip through time! Spartacus will show you interesting events along the way, from the founding of Rome to the end of the empire.

HIT THE TOWN

Put all the name tags in position, then go exploring!

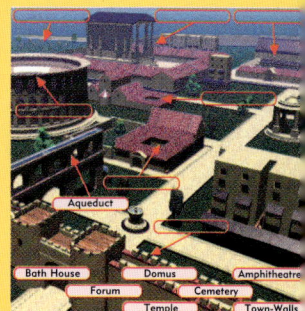

Aqueduct
Bath House
Forum
Domus
Cemetery
Amphitheatre
Temple
Town-Walls

See if you can label the different parts of a Roman town. Find out where the forum was and what a Roman bathhouse looked like.

IN THE PICTURE

Create your own awesome artwork – Roman style!

Here's your chance to make a beautiful Roman mosaic. Pick a template, then choose each tile and put it in position. Once your picture is complete, print it out and keep it!

CONSUL-TATION

Get the answer to all your questions about ancient Rome.

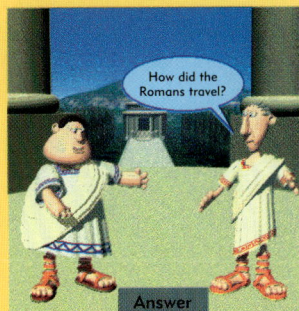

How did the Romans count? What gods did they worship? If you have a question about the Romans, just ask the two wise Consuls. There's nothing they don't know!

WHEN IN ROME...

... you must do as the Romans do!

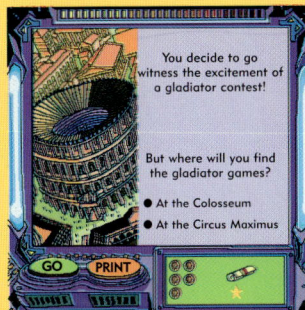

Would you make a good Roman citizen? There's only one way to find out! Let's see if you survive this exciting interactive adventure.

SOLDIER ON!

Can you conquer the mighty empire of Rome?

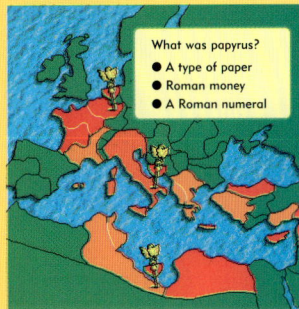

Put your knowledge of ancient Rome to the test! Try to conquer the lands ruled by the Romans in a battle of brain power.

What's in the book

*All words in the text that appear in **bold** can be found in the glossary*

BRITAIN

Londinium (London)

Colonia Agrippina
(Cologne)

Lutetia (Paris)

GERMANY

Rhine

Danube

GAUL

ITALY

Tiber

SPAIN

ILLYRIA

Roma (Rome)

Carthago (Carthage)

MAURETANIA

Mediterranean Sea

The Roman world

According to legend, the Roman civilization began in 753 B.C. Between 300 B.C. and A.D. 200, the Romans conquered a huge **empire**. At its peak, the Roman Empire spanned almost 3,100 miles (5,000 km) from Britain to Egypt. It survived until A.D. 476 and was one of the greatest empires in history.

The Romans built cities and roads throughout their empire. They also taught the people in many of the lands they conquered how to live like the Romans – to wear Roman clothes, worship Roman gods, and speak Latin, the language that the Romans used.

The Romans firmly believed that their own way of life was the best. They thought they were doing other people a favor by showing them the proper way to live.

DISK LINK
Conquer the lands of the Roman Empire when you play SOLDIER ON!

● Byzantium (Istanbul)

MACEDONIA

ASIA MINOR

Euphrates

Tigris

● Athenae (Athens)

GREECE

SYRIA

Hierosolyma (Jerusalem)
●

Alexandria ●   EGYPT

Nile

Goods from all over the empire were brought to Rome by ship. Olives came from Spain, for example, and corn was harvested in Egypt.

9

The city of Rome

At the heart of the Roman Empire was the great city of Rome – home to more than a million people! To many people in the empire, Rome was the center of the world.

The city was full of grand public buildings, such as temples, theaters, bathhouses, and sports arenas. The streets were lined with decorated arches and statues of Rome's greatest leaders.

However, Rome also had many slum districts, where people lived in crowded blocks of apartments separated by narrow, dark alleys.

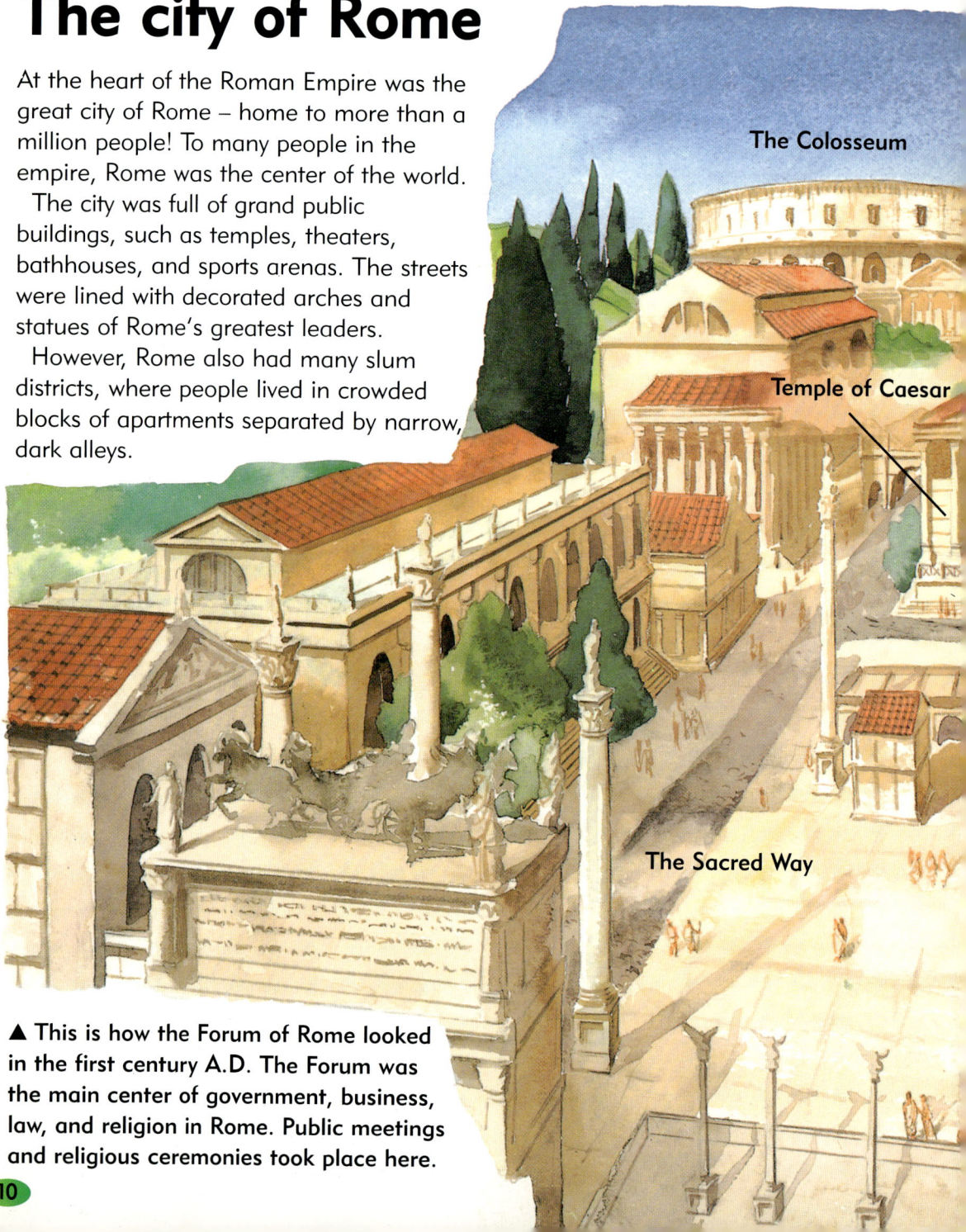

The Colosseum

Temple of Caesar

The Sacred Way

▲ This is how the Forum of Rome looked in the first century A.D. The Forum was the main center of government, business, law, and religion in Rome. Public meetings and religious ceremonies took place here.

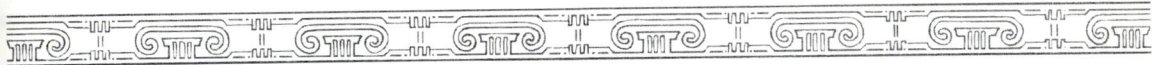

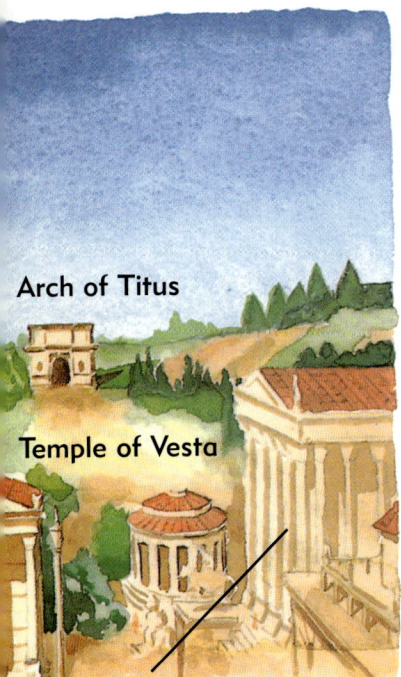

Arch of Titus

Temple of Vesta

Temple of Castor and Pollux

▲ The Forum as it looks today. Can you spot the remains of any buildings shown in the drawing?

Basilica Julia

DISK LINK
There's more to explore when you **HIT THE TOWN!**

VIII

This is how the Roman writer Seneca described the great capital city:

"Look at the crowds! They come here from all over the world. Some come for entertainment, others have come to make their fortunes."

11

Republic and emperors

For almost 500 years, Rome was a **republic**. This meant that it was governed by a group of elected officials rather than by a single person, such as a king or an emperor. Two **consuls** were chosen every year. They ruled with the advice of the **Senate**, a council made up of men from Rome's most important families.

The Republic broke down in a series of **civil wars**. One section of the Roman army battled against another as a group of ambitious politicians and generals fought for power.

The final victor in the civil wars was Augustus. In 27 B.C., he made himself more powerful than the Senate and the consuls and became the first emperor of Rome. Emperors ruled Rome for the next 500 years. There were more than 75 emperors in all.

▼ **Julius Caesar was a successful general and politician. He became ruler of Rome during the civil wars and was given the title *Dictator for Life*. In 44 B.C., he was killed by a group of senators who were afraid he had become too powerful.**

▲ Rome's first emperor, Augustus.

Augustus (27 B.C.–A.D. 14)

Rome was peaceful and prosperous during the reign of Augustus. The Romans admired Augustus so much that after his death, the Senate declared that he had become a god!

Hadrian (A.D. 117–138)

The Emperor Hadrian spent years traveling all over the empire, building forts and walls, such as the one across northern Britain. Hadrian changed some of the laws of Rome to protect slaves from cruelty.

DISK LINK
Meet Caesar, Augustus, and many other powerful rulers of Rome when you take a journey in TIME TREK.

▲ These coins show an emperor visiting London and a new harbor at Ostia, near Rome.

Coins

Roman coins were not just objects for buying things. Many coins had a portrait of the emperor stamped on them. This showed people throughout the empire what their ruler looked like. Coins were also used to announce great events, such as a military victory or a new building.

▲ The Emperor Augustus watches over the building of a new temple in Rome.

The Roman army

It was thanks to the army that the Romans were able to conquer and protect their huge empire. The Roman army was successful because it was better organized, better trained, and better disciplined than any other army of the time.

The army was divided into **legions**, which were units of about 5,500 men. Every legion had a number and a nickname such as *Victorious* or *Lightning*.

A Roman soldier would serve in his legion for up to twenty-five years, living in barracks or a fort with his fellow soldiers. Much of his time was spent training – practicing with weapons or going on long marches loaded with heavy equipment.

helmet with crest

metal jacket

dagger (pugio)

belt (cingulum)

rectangular shield

military sandals (caligae)

short sword (gladius)

▲ An officer's decorated helmet.

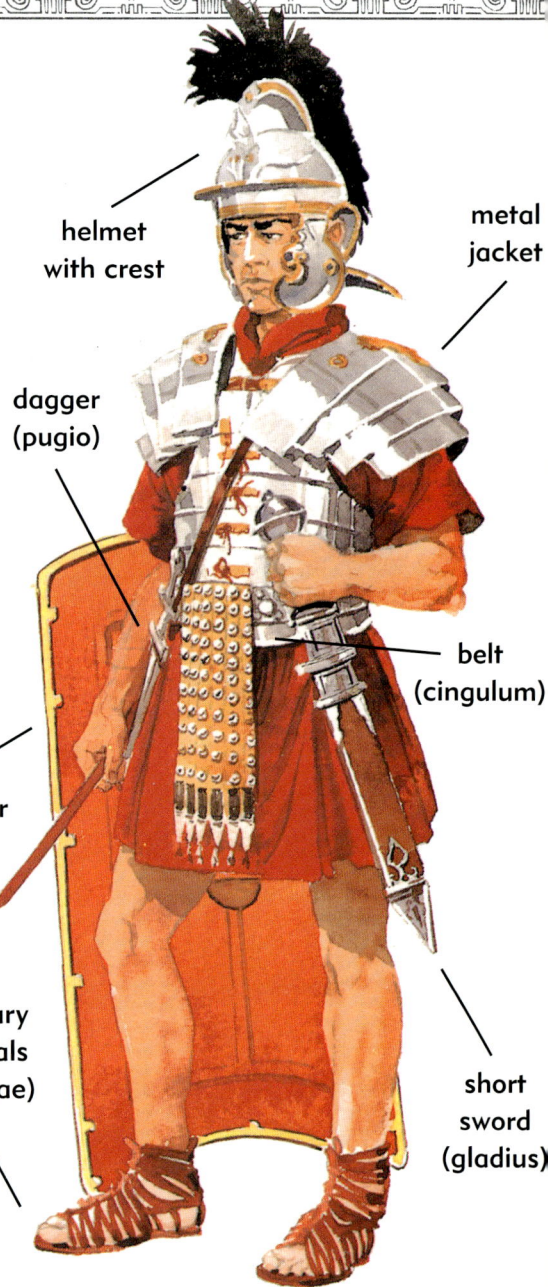

▲ A legionnaire wore heavy armor made of overlapping plates of metal. He wore the helmet crest only on special occasions, such as victory parades.

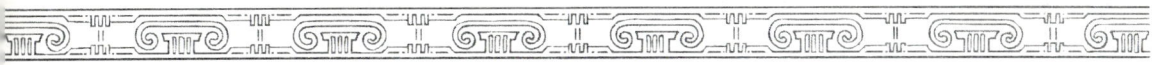

A Roman camp

Most Roman army camps were rectangular. They were surrounded by a ditch and a wall of wooden stakes built on top of a bank of dirt. Inside the camp, the soldiers pitched their tents in neat rows. When they were on the march, soldiers had to build a fresh camp each evening.

DISK LINK
You'll find these pages a big help when you try to put the soldier together in MIX AND MATCH.

Building roads

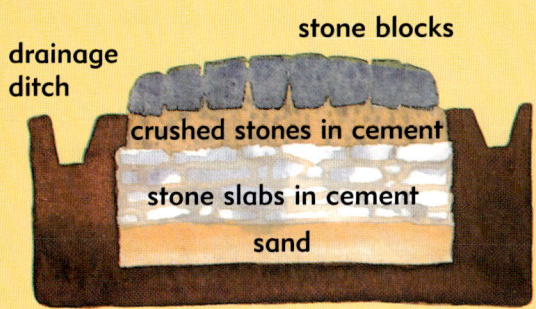

drainage ditch

stone blocks

crushed stones in cement

stone slabs in cement

sand

When they were not training, fighting, or marching, the soldiers built roads. These roads were always as straight as possible, so that the army could travel quickly from one part of the empire to another. The Romans preferred to tunnel through a hill rather than take the long way around it. However, the ordinary soldiers hated road building and grumbled about it in their letters.

Slaves

Roman **citizens** had rights. For example, they were able to vote in elections and were given free corn to make bread. Slaves, on the other hand, had no rights.

Slaves were owned by their masters. They could be bought and sold in the market place and had to work without pay. If they tried to run away, they were often whipped and branded with hot irons, and sometimes even killed.

Some slaves were prisoners, captured in war. Others were the children of slave parents or orphans who had been brought up by slave traders.

Slavery was an accepted part of life in Roman times. Some Romans said that slaves should be treated kindly, but no one thought that slavery itself was wrong.

▼ Wealthy Romans were often carried around by their slaves in small carriages called litters.

▲ Slaves often had to wear metal tags in case they escaped. This one says: "Hold me, if I flee, and return me to my master Viventius."

▲ An African slave pours wine for a Roman.

Gladiators

Some slaves and criminals were forced to become gladiators – men who fought to the death in public entertainments.

These fights were very popular. The crowds would cheer for their favorite gladiators. When the first blood was drawn, they would cry, "He's got him!" Gladiators who won many fights became as famous as film stars are today. But few lived to be old men.

Household slaves

Wealthy Romans had dozens of slaves to help them get dressed, cook for them, entertain them, and clean up after them.

Many slaves came from places outside the empire, such as Germany and Africa. The most highly prized slaves came from Greece, and they were often better educated than their Roman masters! They served as doctors, tutors, and secretaries. Slaves who served their masters well were sometimes rewarded with their freedom.

▲ In addition to fighting each other, gladiators were made to fight wild animals, such as lions and bears.

DISK LINK
The information on these pages will help you to act like a true Roman in WHEN IN ROME.

▲ A gladiator's dagger.

Gods and temples

The Romans worshiped many different gods and goddesses. They believed that each of the gods controlled a different part of their lives. The king of the gods was called Jupiter. His wife, Juno, was the goddess of married women and childbirth.

There were gods for almost every activity, as well as gods for places. There was even a goddess, called Cardea, who watched over door hinges!

DISK LINK
Who were the other Roman gods and goddesses? Just ask the wise Consuls in CONSUL-TATION.

▼ Many Roman houses had shrines. Every day, an offering would be left on the shrine to the gods who protected the home.

▲ This is Serapis, a sun god from Egypt. As the empire expanded, gods from other countries became part of Roman religion.

Christianity

The biggest change to Roman religion was the development of Christianity. The Christians believed in just one god, and they refused to worship the Roman gods. At first, the Christians were punished as criminals. But in A.D. 312, Emperor Constantine converted to the new religion.

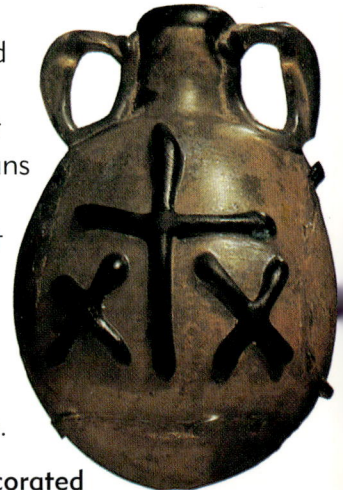

▶ This jug is decorated with Christian symbols.

Signs from the gods

The Romans believed that they could tell from special signs whether the gods were pleased or angry. One popular way of reading the signs was to offer food to a flock of "sacred chickens." If the chickens refused to eat the food, it was a bad sign. In the 200's B.C., a general named Claudius Pulcher took some sacred chickens to sea with him. He was furious when they refused to eat and threw them overboard, crying, "If you won't eat, you'll drink instead!" Soon after, he suffered a terrible defeat. People blamed it on Pulcher's treatment of the chickens.

Roman baths

Every Roman town had at least one public bathhouse. Here, for a small sum, people would come each day to exercise, wash, chat, and relax.

Men and women bathed separately. The bigger bathhouses had special areas for each sex. In the smaller baths, they would bathe at different times of the day.

Each bathhouse had a courtyard for exercise, such as weightlifting, wrestling, or ball games. There was also a swimming pool and a number of rooms that were kept at different temperatures. Bathers sat and sweated in the hot room, where they could also take a hot bath. Then they might move to the cold room for a quick plunge in the cold water.

cold room (frigidarium)

▼ The Romans did not have soap, so slaves massaged the bathers with olive oil, and then scraped the skin clean with a curved metal tool called a **strigil**.

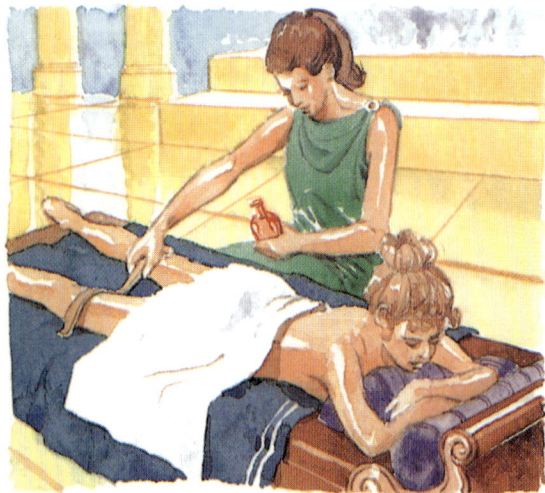

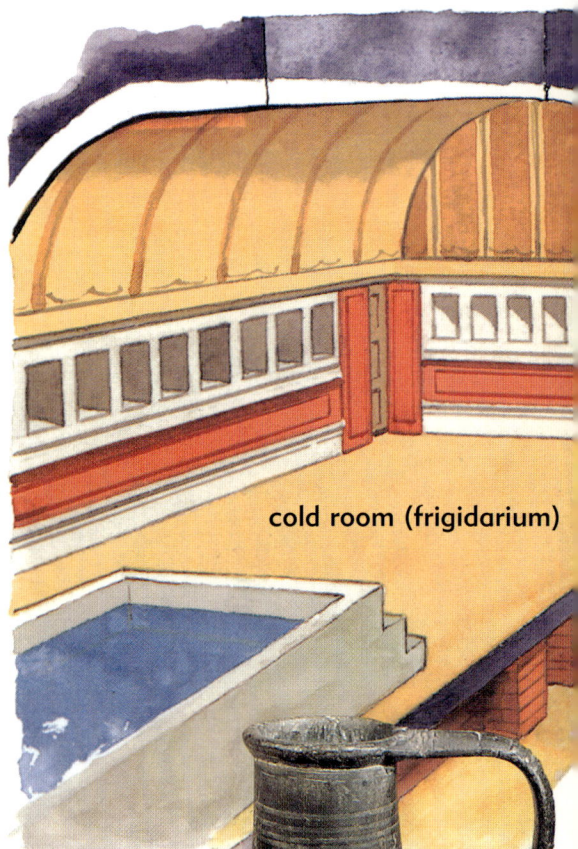

► Many bathers carried their own oil to the baths in jugs like this one.

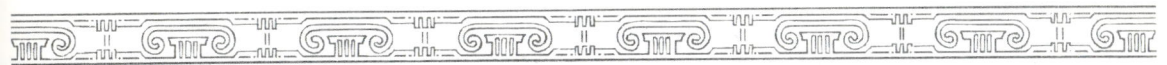

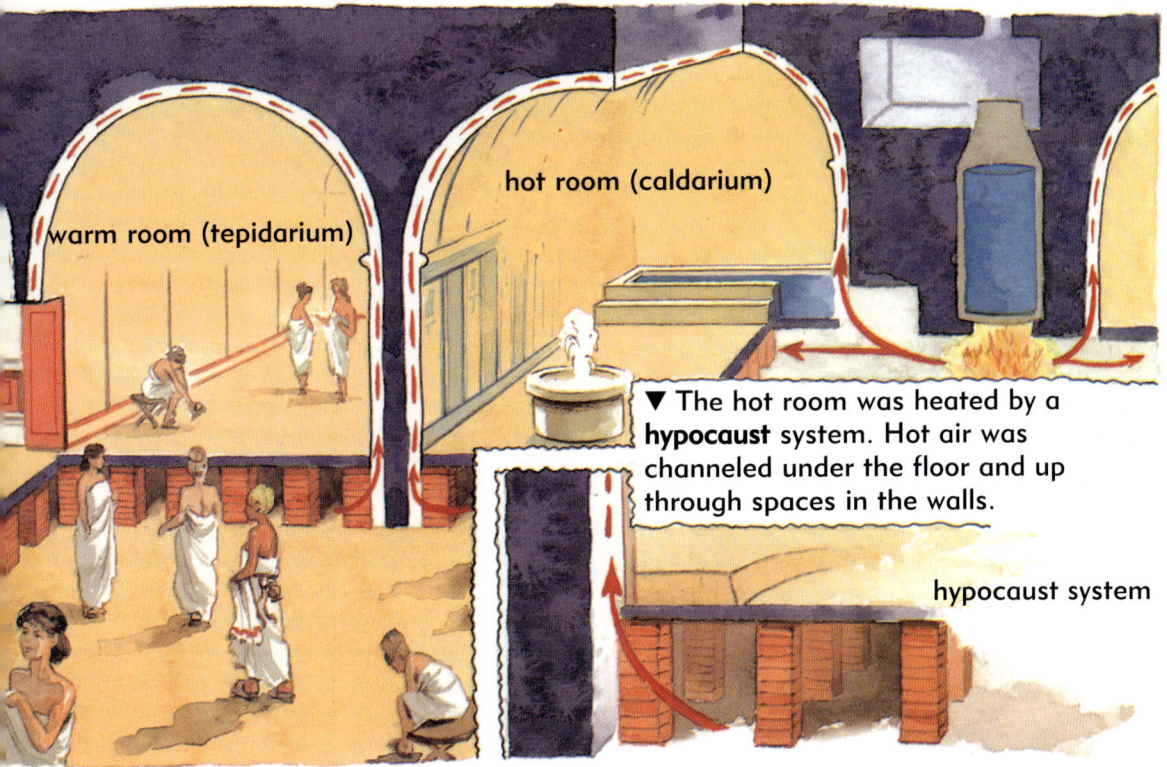

warm room (tepidarium)

hot room (caldarium)

▼ The hot room was heated by a **hypocaust** system. Hot air was channeled under the floor and up through spaces in the walls.

hypocaust system

DISK LINK
Why not spend some time at the baths? You can when you HIT THE TOWN!

VIII

▶ Roman towns used a lot of water. Running water was supplied to the bathhouses and many of the homes. Water was brought to the towns along special arched channels called aqueducts. These carried water from nearby lakes, rivers, and springs. Many of the aqueducts ran undergound, through mountains, and across rivers. Some people secretly piped water into their homes so that they didn't have to pay for it!

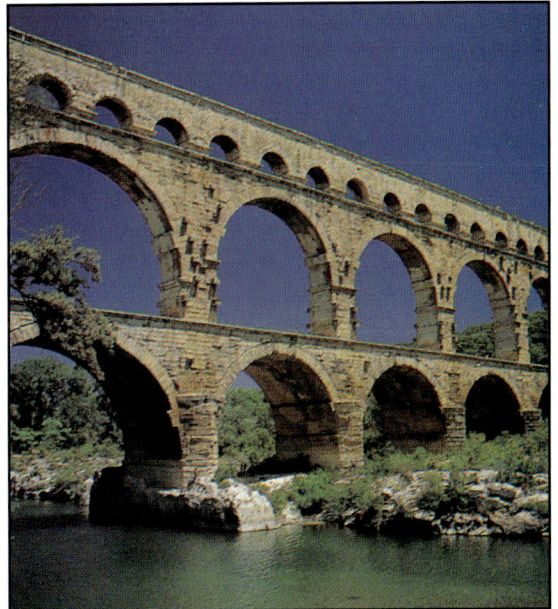

Farming

Most farming was done on large estates that were owned by wealthy Romans. Each estate had a large work force of slaves, watched over by a steward.

The most important crops were wheat, olives, and grapes. Each farm had a building for making wine and presses that crushed olives to make oil. Many farms also had workshops for carpenters and blacksmiths, who repaired the tools and carts.

Slaves looked after the cattle, sheep, and pigs. Oxen were used to pull the plows and the carts that took the goods to market.

▲ Slaves harvested and threshed corn. Horses were then used to trample on it, separating the grains from the husks.

The Romans used pruning knives on their vines and olive trees.

A farmer's sacrifice

Throughout the year, Roman farmers performed religious rituals. In May, for example, a pig, a ram, and a bull would be led around the fields and then killed as a sacrifice to the god Mars. The Romans believed that these rituals were just as important as sowing or plowing.

How to treat your slaves

Roman landowners didn't always agree about the best way to treat their slaves. Some people thought it was better to treat slaves kindly:

"The foremen will work harder if they are rewarded. They should be given a bit of property of their own, and mates from among their fellow slaves to bear them children. This will make them more steady and more attached to the farm."

But other landowners thought that slaves were no more important than the animals on the farm:

"Sell worn-out oxen, worn-out tools, old slaves, and anything else that is no longer of any use."

▼ This **mosaic** shows slaves gathering and stomping grapes to make wine.

Food

Poor Romans lived on a very simple diet of porridge or bread made from wheat, and soup made of millet or lentils, along with beans, onions, turnips, olives, and pork – the cheapest meat.

In contrast, wealthy Romans could afford to buy food from all over the empire. These delicacies included pears from Syria and wine from Greece.

A Roman kitchen

Roman kitchens were usually small, with simple equipment. Food was fried or boiled in earthenware or bronze pots over a charcoal fire. Meat was roasted in the ashes of a small brick oven. The kitchen also had large jars of olive oil, wine, vinegar, and fish sauce, as well as a **mortar** for grinding up spices.

▼ The slaves are kept busy in the kitchen of a wealthy Roman house, preparing a dinner party.

◀ Pottery was mass-produced for Roman kitchens. These bowls were made in Sussex, in southern England.

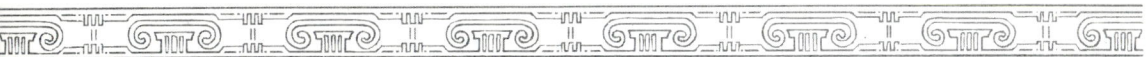

▲ This mosaic shows a slave boy working in the kitchen.

DISK LINK
Find out about a banquet with a difference in CONSUL-TATION!

A dinner party

Serving expensive and unusual food at a banquet was a way of showing off. Guests ate lying down on couches. They picked at the food with their fingers and often had to wash their hands during the meal.

Dinner had a number of courses. It started with an appetizer – salad, eggs, snails, or such shellfish as sea urchins. These tidbits were served with **mulsum**, which was wine sweetened with honey.

Fish and meat dishes were served as the main course. Specialties included dormice stuffed with pork and pine nuts, sows' udders, and roast peacock. The more unusual the food, the better! Finally, there was a sweet course of cakes and fruit.

After the meal, the guests would be served more to drink while they were entertained by storytellers, singers, musicians, and acrobats.

▲ The most popular Roman flavoring was **liquamen**, or fish sauce. It was made from anchovies or mackerel that were soaked in salt water and left to age in the sun. It was very spicy and salty.

A Roman house

From the outside, the houses of wealthy Romans looked quite bare. They were designed to be private and safe from burglars, so there were few outer windows. Instead, Roman houses faced inward, with rooms arranged around a courtyard and a garden.

If you visited a Roman house, the first room you entered would be the **atrium**, a sort of entrance hall or courtyard that had an opening in the ceiling to let in light. Beneath the opening there was a basin to collect rainwater. This basin would have been the family's main water supply.

From the atrium, you would go into the **tablinum**, a sort of living room and office. This was where the head of the family would greet his daily visitors.

peristyle

tablinum

bedroom

atrium

kitchen

▲ A cut-away view of a Roman house

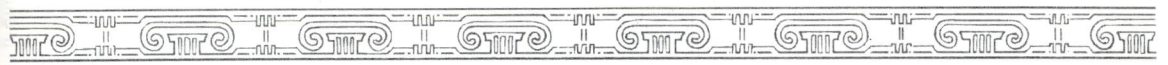

Behind the tablinum was the garden, which was full of flowers and ornamental statues. The most popular type of garden, called a **peristyle**, had a covered walkway around its edges, giving shade on hot summer days.

▶ The Romans decorated the walls of their homes with brightly colored paintings. The floors were often covered in mosaics — pictures made from hundreds of tiny tiles.

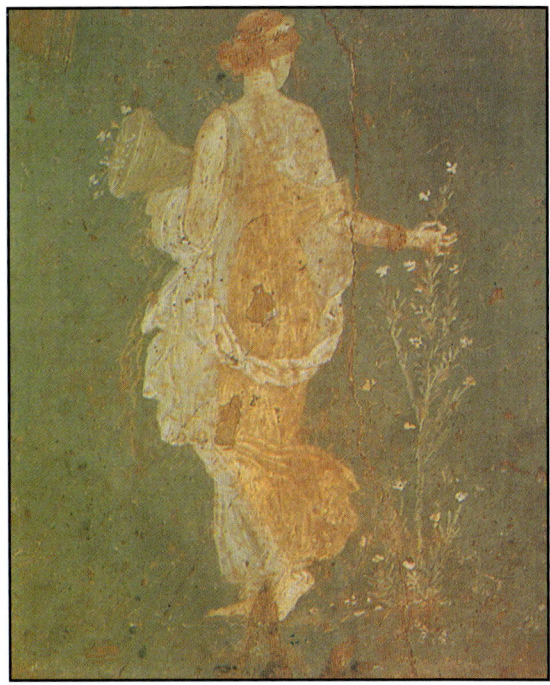

DISK LINK
You can make a mosaic on screen! It's easy when you're IN THE PICTURE.

Make a mosaic

You can make a mosaic yourself, using squares of colored paper instead of real tiles.

● Cut several sheets of different colored paper into small squares.

● Sketch the outline of your mosaic in pencil on a sheet of plain paper.

● Then stick the colored squares in place with white glue.

● Remember to leave a tiny space between each of your paper "tiles," so that the mosaic looks realistic.

Clothes

Men

Roman citizens wore a short wool or linen tunic. Over the tunic, they wrapped a toga – a big, plain, woolen sheet, arranged in a complicated system of folds. The toga was kind of like a suit is today. Men wore togas in public when they wanted to look stylish.

Men were usually expected to be clean-shaven. This meant a painful, daily ordeal at the barber's, for the Romans did not have shaving cream. Even household slaves would be sent off to be shaved. It was a great relief for many men when the Emperor Hadrian decided to grow a beard and made shaving unfashionable.

▼ Rich women wore beautiful jewelry set with precious stones, such as this necklace, bracelet, and brooch.

▲ A wealthy Roman citizen and his wife in stylish dress.

Women

Women wore a much longer tunic that reached down to their ankles. Married women wore a gown with sleeves, called a stola, on top of their tunic.

Women's hairstyles were always changing. Hair might be piled up as high as possible or worn in tight ringlets. Women also wore elaborate wigs. Some were jet black, made of hair imported from India. There were also blonde wigs, using hair clipped from German slave girls.

Romulus and Remus

By the time the Romans began to write down their history,
their city was already centuries old. But they told stories about their early years,
to explain how their way of life had come about. This story explains how
Rome was founded and how it got its name.

Long ago, a wicked king called Amulius ruled over the city of Alba Longa. He had stolen the throne from his elder brother, Numitor, who fled to the hills and hid among the shepherds and herdsmen.

Amulius killed Numitor's two sons and forced Numitor's daughter to become a priestess. That way, she could never marry and have children who could take power away from Amulius.

One day, Amulius was furious to hear that his niece had given birth to twin boys. She claimed that their father was Mars, the god of war, who had visited her one night in a dream. Amulius did not believe her and ordered the two boys to be drowned.

Instead of drowning the boys, Amulius's servants set them afloat on the Tiber River in a reed basket. They drifted down the river, toward the Palatine Hill, where they finally came to rest under a fig tree.

A she-wolf came across the babies, attracted by their crying. Instead of killing and eating them, she looked after the boys, feeding them with her own milk.

Soon after, an old shepherd named Faustulus was watching his flock when he noticed the fresh tracks of a wolf. Taking his spear, he set off to find the animal to kill it. To his amazement, he found the she-wolf with the two baby boys.

Faustulus took the babies home with him and showed them to his wife, Laurentia. The old shepherd and his wife had no children of their own, although they had always longed for some. The couple decided they would bring up the boys and named them Romulus and Remus.

The twins grew up among the shepherds and herdsmen of the hills by the Tiber River. As they got older, the boys displayed such strength and cleverness that people knew they were born leaders.

One day, some herdsmen looking after the flocks belonging to Numitor accused the twins of stealing cattle. There was a fight and, in the scuffle, the herdsmen took Remus as a prisoner.

Numitor was puzzled when he met Remus. Something was strangely familiar about him. When Remus told Numitor his age and that he had a twin brother, the old man realized that he was talking to his own grandson! He was overjoyed. He told the twins who they really were, and how his wicked brother, Amulius, had wanted them dead.

Romulus and Remus agreed to help their grandfather get back the throne of Alba Longa. They led their fellow shepherds to the city and made a surprise attack on Amulius, killing him in his palace. Numitor was then welcomed back by the people of Alba Longa as the rightful king.

The twins now lived as princes in Alba Longa. But they were not happy there. They missed the hills on the Tiber River, where they had grown up. Eventually, they decided to go back there to found a city of their own.

Once they had reached the Tiber, the twins began to argue about where the city should be built. Remus said it should be on the Aventine Hill. Romulus said they should choose the Palatine Hill, where they had been discovered by the she-wolf.

At last, the brothers decided to ask the gods to settle the question. Each of them stood on the hill he favored and watched the sky for birds, the signs from the gods.

Soon a group of vultures began to circle high up in the air. Six of them flew over Remus, who shouted: "Look! The gods have chosen me!"

But then twelve of the vultures flew over Romulus. Romulus began to mark out the boundary line of his city, and his followers started digging a deep trench.

Remus watched with growing anger. He began to shout insults at his brother. For a while, Romulus ignored his brother's taunts, but when Remus and his followers started to jump over the boundary line, Romulus lost his temper. A terrible fight, using picks and shovels, broke out and Remus was killed.

Instead of showing sadness at his brother's death, Romulus just said grimly: "That's what will happen to anyone who tries to jump over my city walls!"

The new city was given the name of Rome, in honor of Romulus. He proved to be a wise king and ruled over his people for thirty-eight years.

One day, while King Romulus was watching his soldiers parade on the Field of Mars, there was a sudden thunderstorm. A thick black cloud wrapped itself around Romulus and, in a flash of lightning, he disappeared. The Romans said that their founder had gone to join his father, Mars, up in the heavens.

How we know

Have you ever wondered how we know so much about the Romans, even though they lived so long ago?

Evidence from books

The Romans were great writers. Many of their books and letters have survived. We can still read Roman poetry, plays, and history books, as well as manuals on law, religion, warfare, farming, and cookery.

▲ Scenes on mosaics like this one tell us many things about life in Roman times.

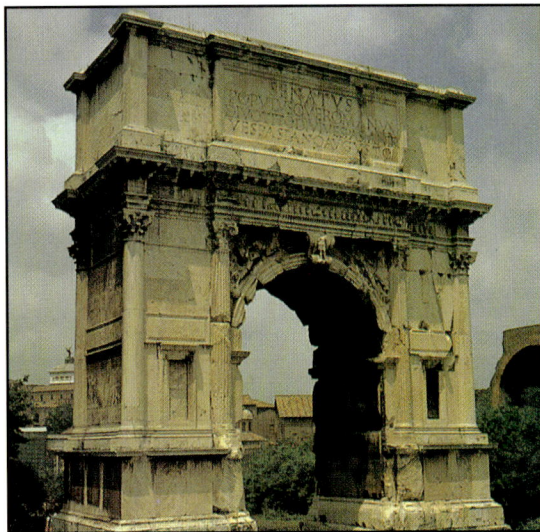

▲ This is the Arch of Titus, in Rome.

Evidence around us

The Roman way of life still influences our lives today. Many of our words come from Latin, the Roman language. Some of the names that we use for planets and months of the year come from the names of important Roman people, or figures from Roman mythology. Many of our buildings, as well as our coins, are modeled on Roman ones.

Evidence from the ground

Archaeologists have uncovered many Roman buildings. The most spectacular discoveries are from the remains of the city of Pompeii. In A.D. 79, the volcano Vesuvius erupted and covered Pompeii in ash and mud. The remains of Pompeii were so well preserved in volcanic ash that even food cooking on a stove before the sudden eruption has been uncovered!

▲ Many people lost their lives at Pompeii. This boy was buried under the volcanic ash. When his body decayed, it left a space in the ash that archaeologists filled with plaster to make a cast.

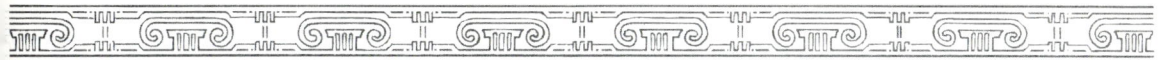

Glossary

Atrium The entry hall of a Roman house.

Citizen A member of a state or nation. In Roman times, only citizens had the right to run for election, vote, or join the legions.

Civil war A war between people belonging to the same nation.

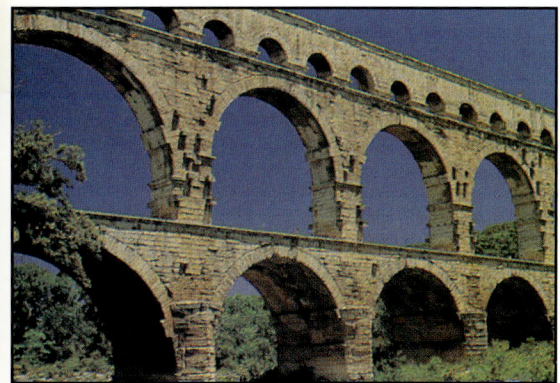

Consuls The two most important officials in the Roman Senate.

Empire A large area containing many lands and peoples, all ruled by one government. In Roman times, the rule of the emperors was also called the Empire.

Hypocaust A type of central heating. Floors were held up on brick columns, and hot air was channeled underneath.

Legion A division of the Roman army, made up of about 5,500 men.

Liquamen A sauce made from aged fish.

Mortar A stone bowl that was used to grind spices.

Mosaic A picture made from tiny tiles.

Mulsum Wine sweetened with honey.

Peristyle The garden of a Roman house with a covered walkway around its edges.

Republic A state ruled by elected officials instead of by a king or an emperor.

Senate The Roman governing council, made up of men from the most important families. It gave advice to the consuls and, later, to the emperor.

Strigil A metal tool for scraping dirt and oil off the skin.

Tablinum The most important room in a Roman house, a reception room and office.

Toga A plain, rectangular piece of material worn wrapped around the body.

Lab pages

Photocopy these sheets and use them to make your own notes.

Lab pages

Photocopy these sheets and use them to make your own notes.

Loading your INTERFACT disk

INTERFACT is available on floppy disk and CD-ROM for both PCs with Windows and Apple Macintoshes. Make sure you follow the correct instructions for the disk you have chosen and your type of computer. Before you begin, check the system requirements on pages 44–45.

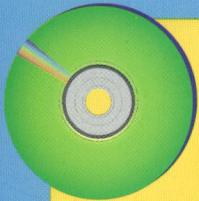

CD-ROM INSTRUCTIONS

If you have a copy of INTERFACT on CD, you can run the program from the disk – you don't need to install it on your hard drive.

PC WITH WINDOWS 95

❶ Put the disk in the CD drive
❷ Open MY COMPUTER
❸ Double click on the CD drive icon
❹ Double click on the icon called ROMANS

PC WITH WINDOWS 3.1 OR 3.11

❶ Put the disk in the CD drive
❷ Select RUN from the FILE menu in the PROGRAM MANAGER
❸ Type **D:\ROMANS**(where D is the letter of your CD drive)
❹ Press the RETURN key

MACINTOSH

❶ Put the disk in the CD drive
❷ Double click on the INTERFACT icon
❸ Double click on the icon called ROMANS

FLOPPY DISK INSTRUCTIONS

If you have a copy of INTERFACT on floppy disk, you must install the program on your computer's hard drive before you can run it.

PC WITH WINDOWS 95

To install INTERFACT:

1 Put the disk in the floppy drive

2 Select RUN from the START menu

3 Type **A:\INSTALL** (Where A is the letter of your floppy drive)

4 Click OK – unless you want to change the name of the INTERFACT directory

To run INTERFACT:

Once the program has been installed, open the START menu and select PROGRAMS, then select INTERFACT and click on the icon called ROMANS

PC WITH WINDOWS 3.1 OR 3.11

To install INTERFACT:

1 Put the disk in the floppy drive

2 Select RUN from the FILE menu in the PROGRAM MANAGER

3 Type **A:\INSTALL** (Where A is the letter of your floppy drive)

4 Click OK – unless you want to change the name of the INTERFACT directory

To run INTERFACT:

Once the program has been installed, open the INTERFACT group in the PROGRAM MANAGER and double click the icon called ROMANS

MACINTOSH

To install INTERFACT:

1 Put the disk in the floppy drive

2 Double click on the icon called INTERFACT INSTALLER

3 Click CONTINUE

4 Click INSTALL – unless you want to change the name of the INTERFACT folder

To run INTERFACT:

Once the program has been installed, open the INTERFACT folder and double click the icon called ROMANS

How to use INTERFACT

INTERFACT is easy to use.
First find out how to load the program
(see page 40), then read these simple
instructions and dive in!

You will find that there are lots of different features to explore.
To select one, operate the controls on the right-hand side of the screen. You will see that the main area of the screen changes as you click on different features.

For example, this is what your screen will look like when you play Consul-Tation, where the consuls will answer all your questions. Once you've selected a feature, click on the main screen to start playing.

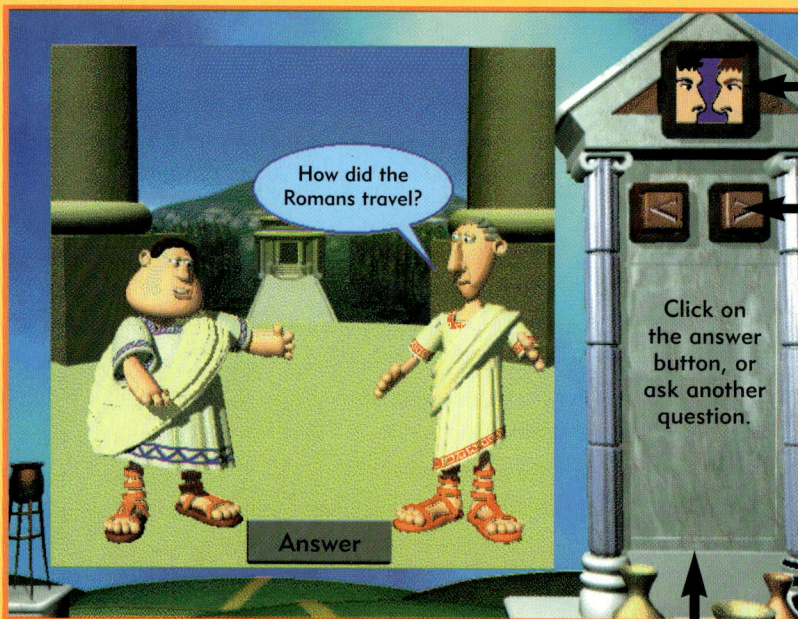

How did the
Romans travel?

Answer

Click here to select the feature you want to play.

Click on the answer button, or ask another question.

Click on the arrow keys to scroll through the different features on the disk or find your way to the exit.

This is the text box, where instructions and directions appear. See page 4 to find out what's on the disk.

DISK LINKS

When you read the book, you'll come across Disk Links. These show you where to find activities on the disk that relate to the page you are reading. Use the arrow keys to find the icon on screen that matches the one in the Disk Link.

DISK LINK
Are you good at organizing people? Then give MIX AND MATCH a try!

BOOKMARKS

As you explore the features on the disk, you'll bump into Bookmarks. These show you where to look in the book for more information about the topic on screen. Just turn to the page of the book shown in the Bookmark.

23

LAB PAGES

On pages 36–39, you'll find note pages to photocopy. These are for making notes and recording any thoughts or ideas you may have as you read the book.

HOT DISK TIPS

● After you have chosen the feature you want to play, remember to move the cursor from the icon to the main screen before clicking the mouse again.

● If you don't know how to use one of the on-screen controls, simply touch it with your cursor. An explanation will pop up in the text box!

● Keep a close eye on the cursor. When it changes from an arrow ← to a hand, ☞ click your mouse and something will happen.

● Any words that appear on screen in blue and underlined are "hot." This means you can touch them with the cursor for more information.

● Explore the screen! There are secret hot spots and hidden surprises to find.

Troubleshooting

If you come across a problem loading or running the INTERFACT disk, you should find the solution here. If you still cannot solve your problem, call the helpline at 1-800-424-1280.

QUICK FIXES Run through these general checkpoints before consulting COMMON PROBLEMS (see opposite page).

QUICK FIXES

PC WITH WINDOWS 3.1 OR 3.11

1 Check that you have the minimum system requirements: 386/33Mhz, VGA color monitor, 4Mb of RAM.

2 Make sure you have typed in the correct instructions: a colon (:) not a semi-colon (;) and a back slash (\) not a forward slash (/). Also, do not put any spaces between letters or punctuation.

3 It is important that you do not have any other programs running. Before you start **INTERFACT**, hold down the Control key and press Escape. If you find that other programs are open, click on them with the mouse, then click the End Task key.

QUICK FIXES

PC WITH WINDOWS 95

1 Make sure you have typed in the correct instructions: a colon (:) not a semi-colon (;) and a back slash(\) not a forward slash (/). Also, do not put any spaces between letters or punctuation.

2 It is important that you do not have any other programs running. Before you start **INTERFACT**, look at the task bar. If you find that other programs are open, click with the right mouse button and select Close from the pop-up menu.

MACINTOSH

1 Make sure that you have the minimum system requirements: 68020 processor, 640x480 color display, system 7.0 (or a later version), and 4Mb of RAM.

2 It is important that you do not have any other programs running. Before you start **INTERFACT**, click on the application menu in the top right-hand corner. Select each of the open applications and select Quit from the File menu.

COMMON PROBLEMS

Symptom: Cannot load disk.
Problem: There is not enough space available on your hard disk.
Solution: Make more space available by deleting old applications and files you don't use until 6Mb of free space is available.

Symptom: Disk will not run.
Problem: There is not enough memory available.
Solution: *Either* quit other open applications (see Quick Fixes) *or* increase your machine's RAM by adjusting the Virtual Memory.

Symptom: Graphics do not load or are of poor quality.
Problem: *Either* there is not enough memory available *or* you have the wrong display setting.
Solution: *Either* quit other applications (see Quick Fixes) *or* make sure that your monitor control is set to 640x480x256 or VGA.

Symptom: There is no sound (PCs only).
Problem: Your sound card is not Soundblaster compatible.
Solution: Try to configure your sound settings to make them Soundblaster compatible (refer to your sound card manual for more details).

Symptom: Your machine freezes.
Problem: There is not enough memory available.
Solution: *Either* quit other applications (see Quick Fixes) *or* increase your machine's RAM by adjusting the Virtual Memory.

Symptom: Text does not fit neatly into boxes and "hot" copy does not bring up extra information.
Problem: Standard fonts on your computer have been moved or deleted.
Solution: Reinstall standard fonts. The PC version requires Arial; the Macintosh version requires Helvetica. See your computer manual for further information.

Index

T

tablinum 26, 27
temples 10, 11, 13, 18
Time Trek 4
togas 28

V

Vesuvius, Mount 34

W

When in Rome 5
wigs 28
wine 17, 22, 23, 25

R

religion 10, 18, 19, 34
Republic 12
roads 9, 13, 15
Roman Empire 12
Rome, city of 10–11, 12, 29, 33
Romulus and Remus 29–33

S

sacrifices 18, 23
Senate 12
shrines 18
slaves 13, 16, 17, 20, 22, 23, 25, 28
Soldier On 5
soldiers 14, 15
stolas 28
strigil 20